MW00573618

Echo Train

AARON FAGAN was born in Rochester, New York, in 1973 and raised in Victor. Educated at Hampshire College and Syracuse University, he has been an assistant editor for *Poetry* magazine in Chicago and a copy editor for *Scientific American* magazine in New York City. He lives near Woodlawn Cemetery in the Bronx.

Also by Aaron Fagan

POETRY
Garage (Salt, 2007)

Echo Train

Aaron Fagan

SALT

LONDON

PUBLISHED BY SALT PUBLISHING
Fourth Floor, 2 Tavistock Place, Bloomsbury, London WC1H 9RA United Kingdom

© Aaron Fagan, 2010

The right of Aaron Fagan to be identified as the
author of this work has been asserted by him in accordance
with Section 77 of the Copyright, Designs and Patents Act 1988.

Salt Publishing 2010

Printed and bound in the United Kingdom by Lightning Source UK Ltd

Typeset in Swift 9.5 / 13

ISBN 978 1 84471 749 1 paperback

1 3 5 7 9 8 6 4 2

to Angela Strassheim

Contents

Acknowledgements

The Alembic: "Moonlore" and "Traffic"

American Poetry Review: "Gym," "Peripeteia" and "Splice"

Dossier: "Yes"

Milk: "Plywood Pterodactyls," "Research and Development," "Side Show and Tell" and "Work Site"

Opium: "Broken Rib"

Shenandoah: "*In Vino Veritas*"

Stand: "Bigfoot," "The Lion-Eating Poet in the Stone Den," "Moonlore," "Ride," "The Source" and "Traffic"

Superstition Review: "No Black Scorpion is Falling Upon This Table"

Tuesday: An Art Project: "A Friday in June"

The Yale Review: "Love"

Echo Train

What we are to our inward vision, and what a man appears to be sub
specie æternitatis *[from the perspective of eternity], can only be expressed
by way of myth. Myth is more individual and expresses life more precisely
than does science. Science works with concepts of averages which are far too
general to do justice to the subjective variety of an individual life.*

— C.G. JUNG

*Centuries of husbandry, decades of diligent culling, the work of numerous
hearts and hands, have gone into the hacking, sorting, and spinning of this
tightly twisted yarn. Furthermore, we have not even to risk the adventure
alone; for the heroes of all time have gone before us; the labyrinth is
thoroughly known; we have only to follow the thread of the hero-path. And
where we had thought to find an abomination, we shall find a god; where
we had thought to slay another, we shall slay ourselves; where we had
thought to travel outward, we shall come to the center of our own existence;
where we had thought to be alone, we shall be with the world.*

— JOSEPH CAMPBELL

*If I spoke, what would it do? — my thoughts mean nothing,
my life means nothing, my death means nothing.
And everything means nothing. Sometimes I sit
here at this bay window and look out
at the field, the hills, the sky, and I see the boulders
laughing, holding their sides and laughing,
and the apple trees shaking and twisting with laughter,
the sky booming and roaring, the whole earth
heaving like a fat man's belly, everything
laughing. It isn't because we're a joke, no,
it's because we think we aren't a joke — that's
what the whole universe is laughing at. It makes
no difference if my thoughts are spoken or not,
or if I live or die — nothing will change.
How could it? The body is wrong, a misery,
a misrepresentation, but hell, would talking make
any difference? The reason nobody knows me
is because I don't exist. And neither do you.*

— HAYDEN CARRUTH

Dramatis Personæ

O NCE upon a time,
Books began this
Way—the O of *once* let
The reader beware up
Front that a story as
Ornate and colorful as
We are would follow—
And not for any of us
To be shocked to find
We must return and
Stand for what we are.

My Entrepreneurial Spirit

While there are parts of me
I cannot put my finger on,
I grow touched that I know

I don't know who I am—
Fighting against all the
Thoughts I keep in time,

Kindred with space, my
Infinite feelings fall out—
Playing night watchman

To the event horizon,
Carving bars of soap into
The clocks I sell as candles.

The Source

The moon has done its part
And it will do its part again tonight
Reflecting light that will illuminate
Our sleep from a source that truly is
On the other side. In this light
It's no wonder that we lie here
Like cattle crowded by the bent visions
Of our dreams. We're better off if the sun
Is the eye of God and not the whole of God—
A single vision that sees everything
And nothing as the same thing.
No two ways of looking at it.
No other version of the self
Going around seeing the future
As a perforated edge along the stars
That can be torn away at any moment
While losing sight of the fact that stars
Burn from their own resources.
Tonight we read from them the story
Of our own light burning—
How the distance it travels is our distance.

Love

Say it's a form of heat that doesn't rise
But passes from one body to the next.
Say it flows through you and then out
And back in again like a ghostly thread
Weaving a basic pattern inside of you
That will slowly begin to take the shape
Of what you'll think you can describe.

Splice

Watching
The moon
Above two
Actors on
Television,
I wonder,
With no one
To turn to,
If I watched
The moon
The night
The moon
Was filmed.

Traffic

Keep your distance.
If you love me, keep
Your distance when
I die — give me room,
But not so much we
Lose sight of the fact
Of our eyes unseeing
Each other vanishing.
Love will be the trust
We were here entirely
And part of this world.
If you put two parallel
Lines down on a page,
Read them carefully.
Look at them sideways,
Draw the meaning into
The distance, and make
A point for departure.

Peripeteia

Polluted with fear, the hour arrives
With the bad faith of saying nothing
Well—keep up your right words,
For the new will trust them: sleep
Is for lunch, and out where the voice
That is still great within us rises up,
Each entity under the sun will map
Their escape route on the back
Of a cocktail napkin before bed—
But who, and how, will we tell it?
Heaven is the color orange you see
When you close your eyes and look
At the sun—but if you could peer far
Enough into the night sky, you'd see
A star in any direction you looked:
When and where will we sleep?
When we find one we can listen to,
But how, and where, it gets out of its
Mystery, and way, we may never know.
Who, but we, did wander through
The murderous chafe of days sublime?

Public Sounds from Afar

I had to see or hear or feel her feet
Waltzing accordion swirls in a swath
On paraded pavement. Or wash them
Relinquished of their sneakers and lick
The ankle as crucial and climb as far
As the material world of her outfit
Would allow from a grand illusion.
Today she stops deeply imagining
She has scouted out some more
Handsome successors. O joy of
Being a friend to the neighborhood.
Of lending a hand. For a single flag,
For the first and last, I am without
Armor or hatred and more serious
Than a widow in repose. Her heart
Is unmoved, but her teeth expose
Their wolf smile. O come my
Beautiful sun. O come my Mexican
Night. Arrive in my eyes, beating
Our countryside. The sky can wake
Up the stars to flower. Tear the flesh
Off yourself. Keep silent. Climb.
Bite. But come! Place your cheek
Against mine. Go down. Tread
Lightly. Cover yourself with light.
Use of threats, use of prayer. We
Haven't finished talking about love.

Glassolalia

Your sentimental sky will undergo no change.
What demons mollycoddle, I invest with poor
Ideas that lean out to whisper sweet nothings at
The *mother* in chemotherapy. I piss my pants
And freeze to the sidewalk. You—still, honestly—
Believe I have the nerves to proclaim the monsters,
The four known forces, are good to me, good to you.
Can you feel your presence in the air? (It felt like it
Was happening.) I will die asleep on a Ferris wheel.
The .10 caliber automaton in me learns to hum a bar,
A laid paper going the fetch length of moot laughter.

Ride

Standing in the shade at sea level,
Who am I to say what a person's
Peace is or will be. I labor at a wish
To court, groom an adequate, fully
Operable oblivion to no avail.
In a few days, crowds come to see.
How can I pronounce willingness
And rhyme watch fob against sob
With a straight face among guests
I've never had the courage to map?
The consequences, the patterns
Of energy recommend: breathing
Deep, inexpensive massages,
Using your finger as a broom
Across the table. Everything
We have at our disposal is gone
And illustrious, I admit to the rain.

Bigfoot

Beneath a curved pine and lost,
One last time before I sleep,
I pull these ancient knees up
To my chin and gesture what
I saw emerge from a blur, out
In the desert, where stones
Have left trails of sand behind.
You can see the sand is fine,
That the desert is flat, but as
The rain comes down at night,
While you are fast asleep, one
Thin sheet of ice forms a plane
And the tension of wind on ice
Moves the stones forward.
There is wind, ice, and stone
In the desert taking thousands
Of years this wonder to perform.
Flow not so fast old mountain.

The Lion-Eating Poet in the Stone Den

When the scepter starts to be an intransigent specter again
It is enough to know it is not enough to know is not enough.
Violence outlasts the ridicule, the dormant actuarial scene's
Super-flat gestures and that stance that increases a *don't just
Sit there and behold it, invest!* kind of an attitude. Sing for
The dying late in the right time. One good thing about your
Meandering concern may be the way we come to be skinned
Alive and suffer all of this, or not at all, in dignified silence.

Moonlore

Knowing what I know now
I don't want to know anymore:
There's a man on Earth selling
Realty on the moon. Legally.
It was bad enough knowing
There are footprints, a flag

And other crap up there just
Waiting for the day to come
Down here when we can go up
To collect and expand, Luna.
You have offered me more
Madness than I can stand,

But bless you for no binding
Contracts or agreements for
There's no reward as great as
Letting go of what I love,
And nothing worse than
Letting go of what I love.

Find a Way for Everyone to Have a Share

Die every day of your life for the fun of it.
Take God out behind the barn to find God.
Let seriousness distort all your passion's
Indigenous surprises. There was a squirrel
Making fun of me when the firehouse alarm
Sounded letting the town know it's noon.
Qualities of light compressed on the back
Window of the car remarkably well—
Playing visual piano to the audible dark or
Easy on the land smears the slug path or
Ceremonies in late aquifer clouds retreat
From taking out justice on the guys
With a hammer drill and the last alpaca.

A New Relationship with God

A little girl has spilled her milk
And she is wailing so loud with
A look of such terror in her eyes
She's done some brand of wrong,
That a serious part of me is serious
And a serious part of me finds this
Hilarious. Since what is emotionally
True is that she is exhausting her
Little humanity as she grapples with
An awkward truth whereas I simply
Imagine the milk is blood and the table
Is the body of a lover who will betray
Her later in life and now all this fuss
Appears to be designed equally, but
I grab her kitten and break it
To demonstrate what I really mean
By suggesting that the milk is blood.

Gym

There is safety around the smell of coffee and laughter.
And a story so simply told it sounds like our story—
Like your life, a lie you made up as you went along—
Until it stopped working, and then you are the hair
Arrested in the shower and won't wash down the wall.
And it's puzzling in the purest sense of puzzling to you—
Inspiration comes in with a dusty tool bag and leaves.
And you wear that "What the fuck?" expression you have
Every time you experience an aspect of relativity like this.
Everything and nothing infinitely like something and never
Left to be what it is or would become begins to sound
Like math for peace—if you just took an involuntary breath
Of hope and surrendered even more to what happens next
And everything you can't imagine after that, with love.
And that is when we doubt and say you'd have to be dead
Or free. The storyteller tells us only our idea of who
We are is dead. And that we are all our own religion.

Side Show and Tell

Three of us sat down at a table
With a redhead and a brunette.
Nothing was being said, so Patrick,
Being Patrick, let them know
I have four toes on each foot.
After a silence the redhead said,
"And I have one leg"—as if we
Were pulling it. So I pulled off
My boots and socks and said,
"See?" to prove it. What felt
Soon, must have been later:
The brunette was upset and left.
And Patrick and what's-his-name
Went their separate ways, alone.
Dancing by the pool table with
A plaid skirt on, the redhead,
Whose name starts with an *E*,
Wanted me to go home with her.
She leaned into me and said
"You couldn't write anything more
Stupid than this, you know?" "Yes,"
Was everything I could say, but I was
Thinking *I love her with all my heart.*
Back at her studio I got undressed
And freaked out by her collection
Of antique robots from the Fifties,
But she was on her bed on the floor
Peeling off her panty hose and I
Poured us each a glass of water.
I walked one over to her as she took
Off her left leg and leaned it against
The radiator until morning.

Work Site

For all the nameless,
Heartfelt expansions,
This quiet boy grows,
Watching the noisy
Village people grow.
Listening to the fancy
Barking of its elders,
He is terribly moved

By all he is lacking
And hides what he
Is lacking and more.
Unlike other, capable
Boys who can relate
To an already existing
Order of this world,
He is, forever, existing

In the same place—
And everywhere else.
"Time," he says, "I
Experience you
And become extinct."
And while he turns
Out to be nothing,
This was a time when

All of time collapsed
And remained with
His illusion, which
Stands in the center
With the carpenter

Hanging from the
Rafters, his unfinished
Sandwich on wax paper.

The Local Talent

Rusty, as you
Can imagine,
Has red, head
And facial, hair.

What you may
Not know is
He drives a
Pickup truck,

Wears dirt-stiff
Overalls and quit
Cooking Tina
A month ago.

Rusty drives,
Blasting whales
Singing their
Thousand-mile

Songs, ignited
In the alone
Position, as so
Often happens,

Looking for
One thing,
Finding
Another.

Research and Development

Captured and pressed and helped
Out of being an apple on a branch,
Slowly the browning juice is put to use
One way—producing multiple effects,
Each more incomprehensible than
The next—unless, from a low airplane
At night, I could watch the thousands
Of channels that are being flashed
Through on televisions with remote
Controls. Then there would be nothing
For me to do but understand that was
A trick my mind was playing on the fact:
That clouds were obstructing the light,
Briefly, from houses on the ground.
And then making paper out of apples
For a living feels reasonable all over
Again, and for no reason whatsoever.

Plywood Pterodactyls

The men with wombs sat down at the bar.
Staring at their long faces in the long mirror,
The world was far away and far more than
Twice of what they saw. Fear, yes, ripped
The doors and the doors of their hearts,
Yes, back and forth. Dust curled in the dirt
Of Main Street whose pavement had been
Exported ages ago, but there was still whiskey
And still more whiskey. Gravity is a lie.
Light is the base hallucination. They dance
For each other and do not know why
And do not care, but do think they do.
Baby St. Jude struts in to show off Scoops—
His stuffed pelican with plastic vampire teeth—
And calls it a swan. We put down our drinks
To praise his advance in weaponizing emotion.

Bellerophon

From a family well versed in the futility of life,
To literally skip earth and jet into the night sky
Was truly visionary when what you did only
Lingered in the heads of men as gods-in-progress.

But, as if anything different could be expected
From a plan involving a wingèd horse aimed
For the kingdom of heaven, a gadfly Zeus sent
Could only punctuate what spurred you on.

The greatest stories are born from fools like
You, an impulse that gives our lives a moment
Ordinary enough to be lived without apologies—
Holding the dark course on a white, bucking page.

No Black Scorpion is Falling Upon this Table

There is only everything.
Each morning I ask if it's the same
At different times and if it's time
To go. Empty the self of self.
Such are the perverse incentives
Of cognitive dissonance. There
She is, silent in a dream I keep
Having where she does this
Elaborate dance number
With a batch of tuxedoed men.
It goes on for hours. Days pass.
I do what I can to not be a danger
To myself and other strangers.
Watch as the world and everything
You love to hate falls away. Way up
High in the sky, no black scorpion
Is falling upon this table. A month
Passes. Like the legal status of a snail,
Number is the ruler of all forms.
I try to teach my children there are
Different kinds of infinity.
Ideas, language, and, of course,
Cogito ergo sum don't make sense
Anymore. Who would have thought
We could make it rich just for liking things.
It's the aspect I fail to consider that rules me.
Spacetime is only very slightly curved,
Except near a black hole. So in practice
You would be swimming for billions
Of years before you moved a millimeter.
I feel and imagine without time, but
Damned myself to a language that demands
I express it there. Backscattered light created
A halo around the shadow of the photographer.
We stand out in the crowd, grabbing

At straws to get it done. The witless
Luck of the periphery. We or I
(Should I feel compelled to say "I"?)
Bend down on one knee and say,
"Same here, same here. I dream only
Of faceless people, too." And all the
Monkeys are healthy now and do not
Glow under normal light. I dropped
My phone in the river today, but
At least I was at the river. Deep within
The idea of good and evil, there is
A magnetism that cancels us out.
When the soul draws near that void,
Life is too empty to talk about.

Dynamic Narrative Archetype

DNA is the tape and proteins make the music.
Before a zygote begins to divide, we are one cell
In a small room with the key of life. And at first,
It all feels like perfect wholeness, but pretty soon
We die without knowing whether it was time
That was short or life that was long. We keep
Reading ourselves as a blueprint and see a world
That is a friend we imagine will live on in our
Reflection but it doesn't. Divided into as many
Selves as there are cells, the division goes on far
Deeper than the first and only memory we have—
A gratitude we mean to make clear more often,
Comes out sideways in houses and philosophy,
Making of a moment, an art of an eternity.

A Friday in June

Your living moment inspires mine
To let go. The noun is not a particle,
But a tighter family of waves. Woman.
The woman this morning at 145th Street
Clearly has cancer and smiles and smiles
At her daughter fussing with her daughter.
Yes, the doors, if they are doors, close.
I imagine our lives together in a heaven
I know nothing about. The young woman
In front of me shares a paragraph from
The introduction to the Mariner edition
Of *The Selected Poems of Anne Sexton*
With her boyfriend and smiles. I want
To point out the poem "The Addict,"
But there isn't time. It's after noon,
The day is almost done. Outside,
A woman with big sunglasses passes.
Golden hair, black and white dress,
A dime bag sticking out of her red
Cummerbund, cell phone the size
Of a calculator held up to her ear.

In Vino Veritas

I dipped my finger into the wine
Placed it on the crystal rim
And with just the right lack
Of pressure I gently followed
The thin resonant line
Pointing to the heart of the thing
With no decipherable center.

Chrome Telegram

Go fuck yourself you fucking fuck.
I would be lying if I told you to.
Or how I loved rain on a hot
Tin barn roof in summer, but,
Otherwise, I may never have
The chance or will to tell you
About the nicotine stains on
My fingers, the smell gasoline
Left in May, my mock theory
Of all the plausible dragons.
All I can say is that I loved
What I didn't understand
Or kings of the past for being
Kings of the past. And the way
Friends translate themselves
Out of uncomfortable laughs
Back into genuine laughter
Without ruining anyone.
What else is there to say
When we are here in praise
Of love and getting quiet
And totally fucking grateful
I suppose and quiet. It is not
Nearly as good as
Go take a flying fuck, but
It will have to do when
I am trying to explain
That I only respect writers
Who use fuck as a period.
Sometimes things get so bad
You consider planting a garden.

Doxy

YOU CAN KEEP EVERYTHING BUT THE AIR
That's the kind of thing I imagine my imaginary
Wife will say when she text-messages our divorce.
Will that be the way it is in your future—where
Separation is cliché it's so terribly fashionable?
When she says THE AIR you might think I think
There is some kind of oxygen problem up ahead.
No. This is based on my fears here and now. And
She will mean THE AIR. Yes, but there must be
Some kind of reason? Yes, but it's only my opinion.
Like a spiritual asshole, everyone has one, and not
Unlike the priest-crafters who have pimped us
Their centuries-worth of bad ideas. This is mine.

Delirium's Elegance

In Paris,
In a life
Before
This one,
I rode a
Stationary
Bicycle in
The cellar
Of a salon
To keep
Hairdryers
Running
Upstairs,
Through
Electricity
Shortages,
Just after
The war,
For Dior.

Lost and Found in 1971

If you find yourself
Running scared for
The first time, here

Is a word game you
Can play that starts
With whole words.

You will roll out 21
Word cubes to piece
Them in sentences:

My heart is with the
Girl now and *I want*
To walk with you.

Yes

To the snow that fell earlier today
And kept me from diving inside,
Where yesterday is a warm country
Thousands of miles away from here—
Footprints get me giggling about how
Temporary all of my arrangements are
And that my feet are adding a few steps
Against the idea that I am a spare part
Of this day I am too scared to live in.
And, Yes, because it feels special to feel
Like nothing special, and in particular,
In boots, on a sidewalk, late in winter.

Broken Rib

I don't want to have my picture taken
Reading porn on a toilet, masturbating
For America at a dump in a HAZMAT suit.

But before the day is done it may come
Down to people walking straight up
To me in order to say, "I don't know
What's wrong with you, but it shows."

And I will want to curl up into a ball,
Until I become nothingness, and say,
"I'm not much, but I'm all I think about."

After Malaika got out of the shower,
I did manage to write down the date
And time she said, "Every time I put
On deodorant it just makes me laugh."

Below that Tracy called after she got
Drunk and fucked a stranger: "I didn't
Not want to come home and be with you."

I admitted it all over the phone to Sarah
In Chicago who has *Lakshmi* tattooed
In Sanskrit just below her left breast
When it was about time I told her,

"I no longer comprehend the meaning
Of joy, but I can still sense a tenderness
Forming in the shadows of your oranges."

Twice she quoted her favorite line of the *Gita*
"I am Time grown old to destroy the world."
I told her a girl from Toronto emailed today
To tell me her "legs are famous in Japan."

Coming To Grips

Grips, unless they're saving, were meant to be broken.
So I abandon the heart of every matter and launch
A decoy of my faith in words so some brand of mercy
May return without being too obtuse to believe in.
Having laid waste to the givens in the equation of me,
I search for a warm law full of beautiful lies

And curious ways that confirm that what lies
In meaning can only come from what's been broken
Down by a gross process of eliminating me
In a net letting go of the past before I launch
The confidence game I play in
Trying to cram myself to the hilt with mercy.

But in all the reasons to play the game of mercy
There are as many that say these words are lies
I build around myself to place my faith in.
All my pledges and promises come up broken
Only to be reassembled in a phrase that will launch
Some other bastardized improvisation called *me*.

Versions are the last thing to trouble me—
Provided they are born from the spirit of mercy.
I'm sure some old self would never think to launch
Much beyond the spirit of lies
That aim for the heart to be broken
Up and watch patiently as the chest caves in.

There is nothing left or at least new to believe in
Which is over half the reason why I am sick of me
I can no longer tell what or if anything is broken
But what I feel and see is cloaked with mercy.
Does this help me believe the whole lot of lies?
No. But it gives me a direction to launch

Out in. It is peaceful to think I'd launch
In the very direction of what I want to believe in
Even if it is another one of the self-told lies
I seem to have grown into the habit of telling me
But to think of it this way gives me hope that mercy
Is a faithful back that won't be broken.

There is no turning back once the silence is broken.
I've grown faithful to my love affair with lies
And abandon at least this way to pray for mercy.

Dum Spiro, Spero

I go on and on about
What it's like to be here —
Taking in and giving back
The complications that
Fill my heart with a sense
Of what desire might mean
When I introduce it to hope —
And for what little wisdom
I have to work with, I breathe,
Like everyone else — inventing
My reason to stay out of thin air.

Meaning

Reason knows nothing
Of the heart's reasons
For allowing ourselves
To play this confidence
Game we play so freely.

Victor

Back in the town
Where I began,
I confess outside

The church
I was baptized in,
That, for now,

I no longer have
What it takes
To take my life.

Blind Infants

What flavor is sweet and oblique?
Heavy are the increases that come
To pass and attest. Like myself, you
Need to be opened. Some were evil,
But we all danced naked as jaybirds.

Millennia ago I packed hand organs,
Calliopes and music machines inside
The walls: my father put enormous
Emphasis on hands, an imperative
Necessity of keeping them neat, clean,
In shape for tending the electric hearth.

This is the way it was: the helicopter
Passenger was a mouse that acted as
Its pilot at the same time. At times
I danced with a fish, a goat without
Horns skins a black cat with its teeth.

Rubbish Heap

One ocean gave, in my dream,
Response to what our moon
Called into question ages ago

And rose, once more, across two
Bare, star-crossed, world-weary
Lovers laid out on inland grass —

Hearts, world-hurt and hard, let
Slow molting passion go to say,
"Distortions, in time, die away."

Panopticon

Until the interruption grows static creases
We will have to sit here and wait. Wait.
And outstanding echoes are occasioning
Outstanding rings of reverb from one future
To another and ours, the future of the past
Rested in their hands and ours. Nothing is
Going top speed when you put it that way.
Given to mood after mood, passed around
Like a pack of wild cigarettes, breathing.
Draw a line and one to keep it company.
Plough through your life and strangers.
I fight with myself and other strangers
And I can't remember, when was I told
To go down for the count, or on you? Do
You no longer want these words to be
Written? Or must we all hold hands and
Insist ourselves on, tear-shackled at dawn
In the wilderness all on the sound of our
Lover's name? Men barfing out their
Self-as-cunt sketches in a brutal panoply
Of cheerfully Fordist conventions.
Temptation strikes its matches against
The bone and invests each scrap of flesh
With unmitigated harmony and rage.
Grueling. A marmalade of marrow boiled
And candied down to ease the shakes.
You must endure. Raise the belly. Flex
Your nostrils out and lose yourself fast
Despite a hell of who-are-you eyes.
I am not the piece of paper I forgot to
Mention. The notebook battles ended
In a whimpering mess of eyes darting

To devour and discover the little sense
That's left to be made on a train ride—
Not for the lack of it, but for the fact that it
Has all come to sound too much like we
Walk our separate ways and do not say,
"Hello!" I am not going to get even.
Will you? Tearing/tearing up, dancing
In roaring pain or to pouring rain, to
The Gordian Knots of hows and whys?
An uncommon sense tells us that our
Lives are brief and relentless eternities
Of power rolling powerless on their
Way between glimpses of light. A lone
King goes mad from square to square.
This is not a batch of pionic fabulism.
We couldn't even tell you what time it is.

Echo Train

A glorious dream! though now the glories fade.

— Goethe, Faustus

Committed to a toy machine aboveground,
I can no longer see the more the past drains
Over and into me as it would a tool to cut.
It lends to the expression: Pass forth, freely.
Hearing out an estatescape of smiles and
Coordinated handshakes, nodding to recover
And depart to return, giving off its pangs,
And its collapses, and its releases — a bundle
Of luck we try to embrace the passage of —
A fountain of youth takes up a collection
Pool, in medias res, when the work of drafting
A policy in the marsh is done. The feeling
Of the forward, irrevocable flow of time
Is a fluke. I was once an insane asshole, too.

Distant future, distant past — overall, these
Are the same. Time's arrow is a heart: the
Length from the tip of the hand to the heart.
Not all of us will have to learn the French for,
"No, black holes are not about to de-story us,"
But this bit is about the width of an avocado
On the moon, as seen from earth. It's not
Always this way. Depending on the days
My shoes will last a day. Maybe two days.
I wake to go out to say hello to the grasses
I weave. And people and the dirt. I rub
The dirt in my hair. Indoors, you told me
To put water on some carrots and I obeyed.
Another thing I couldn't quite explain.

Reason in the canary wavers. You will be
Learning more. Lightning spits back. Imagine,
Floating there, hypnotizing a pocket square,
Having it do whatever you want it to do. You
Can have it escape from a jar. You can have it
Change color, dissolve a knot and more:
Appear and disappear, in and out of somewhere
And nowhere. With beautiful, pathologically
Suspended disbelief, we can be cheap enough
To burn out in a festival of panic over eternal
Nutrition. Or, though our deeply flawed ideas
Persist, we can unveil what an array has led us
To be so allergic to our space and our time, and
It must lie a helpless log upon the waves.

Reference

Putting it in words committed to the page
Is one way we arrest one take on a wavelength
Of daily life, and—in a way—die premature.

That we could have gone any way we choose
Baffles the senses. One comes to feel their limit
With a specific shame, a kind of exacting guilt.

But how is it all possible among possibilities?
We deny the corpse in exchange for the sun.
And the sun for its additives—a certain rightness

In the wrong becomes apparent only in the filth
Illuminated. We have long been coming to pause
And admire the mess we have made like children

Pointing into the toilet for their mothers.
And that is just one of the infinite ways we boast
And drag all of this atomic trash around, and ours—

What is the need in me to want to name this?
Is it even polite to say becoming or begoing?
I am voiced by forces I do not understand.

Concordance

Minding my business
I was reading a poem
Sitting on the toilet.

I got an unexpected,
Conspicuous joy from
Reading the poem.

Come to think of it
I can hardly recall
What the author said.

For reasons I can't
Explain, it was
The word *explain*—

I could feel it being
Inverted by my eyes,
Offered to the brain

In quiet supplication.
I understood I knew
Nothing about this

Little monument
Called *explain,*
But the purity

Of that engagement
With a single word
On paper had me

Feeling all fucked up.
I wiped my ass with
History in mind.

I began to mourn for
The stories our stories
Are in the place of.